MINKY
MASTERY

AuthorHouse™
1663 Liberty Drive
Bloomington, IN 47403
www.authorhouse.com
Phone: 1 (800) 839-8640

Published by AuthorHouse 08/18/2017

ISBN: 978-1-5462-0506-7 (sc)
ISBN: 978-1-5462-0505-0 (e)

Library of Congress Control Number: 2017912858

Print information available on the last page.

authorHOUSE®

MINKY
MASTERY

Billie Veerkamp

Introduction to Minky Mastery

Piecing with Minky fabric requires a few extra steps that most cotton quilters aren't used to thinking about. The edges of Minky have a tendency to curl or stretch. Then when you try to press the seams open they won't press with a crisp straight seam. I have found a way to combat this problem, it takes a few extra steps, but the end product is so worth it.

I use very light weight fusible stabilizer cut into 3/4 inch width by 60 inches in length and fuse it to each (wrong side or back side) of the cut Minky. This will turn the edges of the pieces into non-stretching sewable edges that are easy to manage. I also like using a steam iron with a teflon plate. The teflon plate makes it easier to clean off any sticky buildup from the fusible Pellon.

Lets talk about how to cut the fusible stabilizer. I like using Pellon fusible 820 quilters grid because of the weight and having the preprinted grid helps when I use it for applique. I measure out 60 inches and then recut the Pellon into about 1/2 inch to 3/4 inch wide by the 60 inch length strips. The key here is to make sure that you are cutting the length on the strip so that there is NO stretch. You really want to make sure your pieces are 60 inches long. As you get used to this method you will find that you will probably use 1/2 wide strips without much worry. Your seam allowances are typically 1/4 inch on most projects and 1/2 inch wide by 60 inches in length will be plenty wide enough.

If you plan your project a little ahead you will see how easy this will work. When I am starting a new pattern, I try to calculate how may strips of each color I will need first. As soon as I have cut my strips, I will iron on the fusible to each edge of the wrong side of the fabric before I do any sub-cutting.

This makes the preparation time go fairly quickly. You can iron the Pellon onto the backside of Minky without a presser sheet If your iron is not too hot, but beware, you cannot iron on the from side of this fabric without using a presser sheet. Always test the heat of your iron on a corner of fabric to check. This is a very important tip, use a presser sheet when in doubt. You never want to ruin any fabric by burning or scorching it.

By only pressing stabilizer onto the edges you won't compromise the extra softness of the fabric that we have come to love. Hopefully this technique will allow you to use this amazing fabric in new and creative ways.

One more time saving trick is about pinning. As we all know Minky tends to slide around and we usually have to pin a great deal. You can pin a little or a lot. When sewing long strips in a strata, pin at the top of two pieces being joined and align the edges. Hold them together by pressing your fingertips along the edge while the machine is feeding the fabric through the feed dogs. You will find this amazingly useful. By having the the stabilizer on the edges and this technique will have you sewing this soft wiggly fabric with ease.

Have great fun with this technique
Billie Veerkamp

The Turtle Family

MATERIAL LIST

Roller cutter - new blade
6 yards- Pellon fusible quilters grid 820
Iron
Pressing sheet
60 degree equilateral 12 inch Triangle ruler
36 x 6 inch Minky ruler
Pins
Matching thread
1 light brown fabric marker
1 medium green fabric marker

1 1/2 yard - Azure
1 yard - Topaz
2 yards - Opal
1 yard - Aqua
1/2 yard dark green tie dye turtle shells
1/2 yard sage green for turtle body

Backing - 6 yards Aqua Minky

Cutting directions

Cut 1 yard of fusible Pellon and set aside for the turtles appliqué
Subcut the remaining 5 yards fusible Pellon into 3- 60 inch lengths
Subcut each piece lengthwise into 3/4 inch by 60 inch pieces.
Make sure that the cuts are lengthwise and have no stretch.

Cut each of the Minky colors into 2 1/2 inch wide by WOF (width of fabric).

You will need **11 strips** - 2 1/2 inch wide by WOF pieces of **each color** (Azure, Topaz, Opal, Aqua).

Cut 6 - 2 1/2 inch wide strips by WOF of Azure for inner border, prepare with Pellon stabilizer strips and set aside.

Cut 6 - 5 1/2 inch wide by WOF of Opal for outer border, prepare with Pellon stabilizer strips and set aside for later.

Now before we get to sew the strips, each strip needs to be prepared with a fusible stabilizer piece on each edge on the wrong side. Iron one strip on each edge on the wrong side as shown.

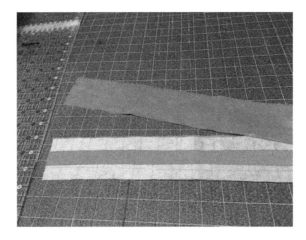

After all the strips are prepared with stabilizer, sew Azure, Topaz, Opal and Aqua into a strata. Sew each strip alternating directions to keep the strata straight using a 1/4 inch seam allowance.

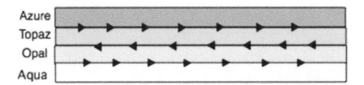

You will have 11 strata groups in the above colors. Now its time to sub-cut the strata into triangles. Using the 60 degree unilateral triangle ruler. Each Strata will provide 5 dark top triangles and 5 light top triangles. Keep the dark tops in one pile and the light tops in another pile. Each triangle will be 8 1/2 inches tall.

You should have created 11 strata sets- this will produce 55 dark bottom triangles and 55 light bottom triangles. The triangles need to have a stabilizer strip ironed on to each edge.

We need 52 dark triangles and 52 light triangles for the quilt. The Triangles will measure 8 1/2 inches tall. Iron stabilizer on each edge of each triangle after you have cut them.

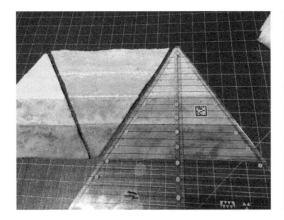

The Quilt top has 8 rows, two dark rows, two light rows, two dark rows, two light rows.

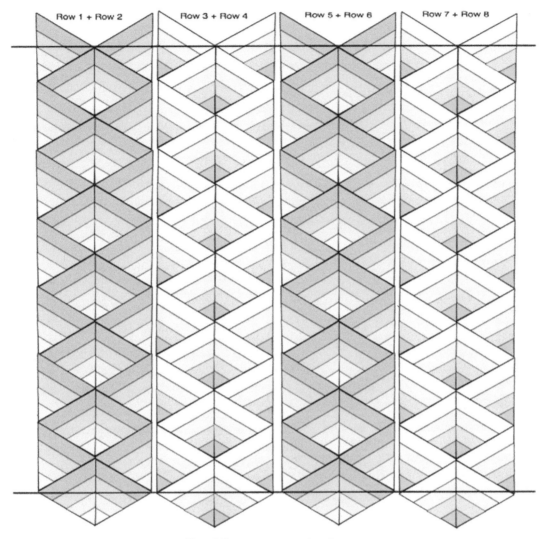

Row 1 + Row 2   Row 3 + Row 4   Row 5 + Row 6   Row 7 + Row 8

After all the rows are sewn together,
draw a chalk line across the bottom

Cut 2 the inner border Azure pieces in half and sew one onto the end of each of the four remaining 2 1/2 inch by WOF inner pieces. This will create 4 pieces about 90 inches long. Measure your sides, you should be 64 inches. Pin and Sew inner border sides, press open with presser sheet. Then measure top and bottom you should have 67 1/2 inches. Cut top and bottom inner borders, pin in place and sew, press open seam allowance with presser sheet.

Now the outer border. Cut two of the Opal 5 1/2 pieces by WOF in half. Sew each half onto the end of remaining 4 pieces. Measure the sides, you should be 65 3/4. Sew and press open. Measure top and bottom, 77 1/2 inches, sew and press open.

This is where you have a choice. I quilted the quilt using 6 yards of Aqua backing before adding the swimming turtles. I made sure my batting was 8 inches larger than the quilt top so that I could wrap the backing over to the front instead of adding binding. This method allowed me to have a 6 inch smooth border on the front and back.

You may sew or applique the turtles onto the quilt top before or after quilting.

Applique instructions

Now take the half of the yard of stabilizer you set aside and trace the turtle body and the baby turtle bodies on half of the stabilizer. Now iron the stabilizer in onto the sage green Minky and cut out your pieces. Trace the turtle shells onto the other half of the stabilizer and iron onto the dark green Minky.

I made 2 big turtles and 12 baby turtles.

Place your turtles swimming across the ocean, Pin them in place and sew around the outside. The great thing about Minky is that it will never fray. Sew the turtle shell lines and flipper marks. You can use the fabric markers to highlight the flipper marks and the outlines of the turtles. Fabric Markers are permanent, test them on a scrap first.

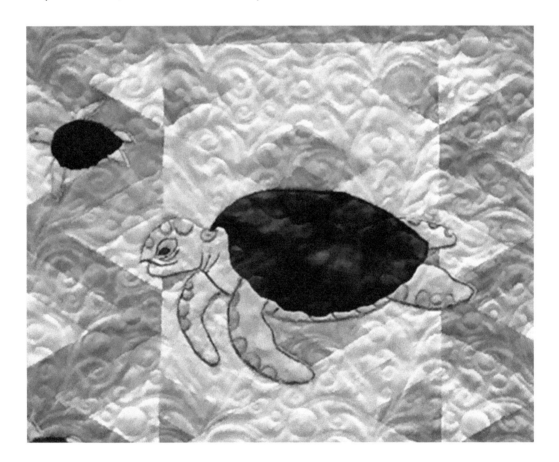

Northern Lights

This quilt was inspired by the Northern Lights that shine once in a while in Montana. As you look to the horizon you can watch the lights flicker through the trees. The Northern Lights are truly magic.

Material List

1/2 yard Turquoise	1/2 yard Dark Purple	1/4 yard Dark Lime
1/2 yard Peacock Blue	1/2 yard Amethyst	1/4 yard Lime
1 yard Midnight Blue	1/2 yard Violet	1/4 yard sage
1 1/2 yard Electric Blue	1/2 yard Jewel	1/4 yard celery
1 1/2 yard royal Blue		
2 yard black		

6 yards Pellon fusible stabilizer
Iron
Pressing sheet
60 degree equilateral 12 inch Triangle
36 x 6 inch Minky ruler
Pins
Matching thread

Cutting Directions

Cut 1 yard of fusible Pellon and set aside for the tree appliqué
Subcut the remaining 5 yards fusible Pellon into 3- 60 inch lengths
Subcut each piece lengthwise into 3/4 inch by 60 inch pieces.
Make sure that the cuts are lengthwise and have no stretch.

Sub cut directions continued

Sub cut each of the following color strata into 2 1/2 wide by WOF-set any remaining fabric aside for later sub cuts.

6 strips - 2 1/2 inch by WOF each of Black, Midnight Blue, Royal Blue, Electric Blue

3 strips - 2 1/2 inch by WOF each of Midnight Blue, Electric Blue, Peacock Blue and Turquoise

3 strips - 2 1/2 inch by WOF each of Dark Lime, Lime, Sage, Celery

4 strips - 2 1/2 inch by WOF of each Dark Purple, Amethyst, Violet and Jewel

Subcut remaining Midnight Blue 2 strips - 8 1/2 inch by WOF

Subcut remaining Royal Blue- 2 strips - 8 1/2 inch by WOF

Subcut remaining Electric Blue 5 strips - 2 1/2 by WOF set aside for binding

Subcut remaining Black - 3 strips - 8 1/2 inch by WOF

Subcut remaining Black - 2 strips - 2 1/2 inch by WOF set aside for binding.

There should be about 26 inches of Black left over set this aside for the tree appliqué.

Additional Subcut for Black 8 1/2 in wide -

After preparing the strips with stabilizer on the wrong side of each edge, sub cut 16 triangles and set aside. We will use these at the ends of the color strata to create the illusion of the ground. Leave the remaining 8 1/2 inch wide black fabric for the border.

Now the prepping begins! Iron one strip of Pellon along each edge of the wrong side of each strip you have cut. Test the heat of your iron before you begin, you don't want it too hot or it will scorch.

After the strips have been prepared, sew each of the color strata using a 1/4 inch seam allowance. Sew the Strips in alternating directions to keep the strata flat and avoid being warped.

Sew strips in alternating directions

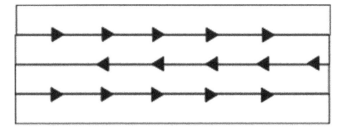 

Purple Strata - Dark Purple, Amethyst, Violet, Jewel (sew 4 sets)

Green Strata - Dark Lime, Lime, Sage, Celery (sew 3 sets)

Turquoise Strata - Dark Turquoise, Peacock, Electric Blue, Midnight Blue (sew 3 sets)

Dark Blue Strata - Electric Blue, Royal Blue, Midnight Blue, Black (sew 6 sets)

Cutting the Triangles-Use the 60 degree triangle ruler. After you have cut the triangles, set the dark bottom triangles in one pile, and the light bottom triangles in another pile.

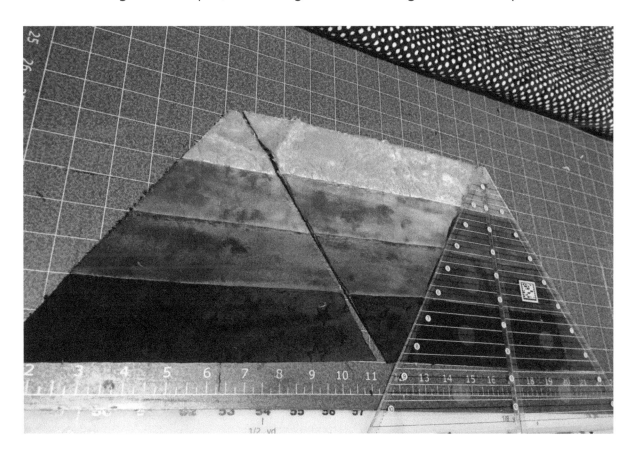

One more step before we get to sew the rows. Now the triangles are cut, we need to iron on a stabilizer to the sides. This step allows a bias edge to be easy to control and sew.

One last group of triangles to make before we sew the rows. We need 8 black triangles.

Take one 8 1/2 strip of Black and create 8 triangles the same way you made the strata triangles. Iron on the stabilizer to the sides of the triangles, just like you did to the strata triangles.

After all the rows are sewn together, draw a chalk line and cut straight across the top and bottom to square up the quilt.

Now we are going to add the bottom border of black. Measure along the bottom, you should have a 64 1/2 inch measurement. Sew two Black 8 1/2 by WOF strips together. Cut to the width of the bottom, (64 1/2 inches) and sew it to the bottom.

Take the remaining black piece and sub cut it into 2 - 18 1/2 inch pieces. Now create the side border by adding the 18 1/2 black piece to a 60 1/2 inch x 8 1/2 inch of midnight blue piece (create 2). Sew to each side.

Now measure across the top, it should measure 80 1/2 inches. Take two 8 1/2 by WOF of the Royal Blue and sew them together. Sub cut the top to 80 1/2 inch and sew along the top.

Sew two of the black binding strips to the remaining 5 strips of Electric Blue. If you begin pinning the binding to the side black and continue allow the bottom the binding will follow the same colors as the border and will add to the illusion of the night sky.

Applique Instructions: Take the 1 yard of Pellon Stabilizer you cut off and set aside . Cut the stabilizer so that you cover as much of the 26 inch x 60 inch pieces of the remaining black Minky. Trace out the outline of the tree on the back of the stabilizer piece that you ironed on to the back of the minky fabric. Pin your tree trunk in the middle and start adding branches. Sew around the outside of the branches with straight or zig-zag.

Quarter Square Log Cabin

OVERSIZED Queen Quarter square Log Cabin

99 1/2 inch x 99 1/2 inch

FABRIC REQUIREMENTS YARDAGE

DARKEST RED	1/4 YARD	DARKEST RED	1/4 YARD
LIGHTEST TAN	1/2 YARD	OFF WHITE	1/2 YARD
MEDIUM TAN	1/2 YARD	CREAM	1/2 YARD
MEDIUM BROWN	3/4 YARD	BEIGE	3/4 YARD
DARKEST BROWN	1 YARD	TAUPE	1 YARD

DARKEST RED ½ YARD INNNER BORDER
TAUPE 1 YARD OUTER BORDER

BACKING – 6 YARDS	5 YARDS PELLON STABILIZER
BINDING- ½ YARD	6 INCH X 36 INCH MINKY RULER

Number Of Strips- All Block Strips 2 1/2 Inch By Wof

1st Color - DARK BROWN BLOCKS

A1	DARKEST RED	1/4 YARD	2 STRIPS
A2 AND A3	LIGHTEST TAN OR CREAM	1/2 YARD	5 STRIPS
A4 AND A5	MEDIUM TAN	1/2 YARD	7 STRIPS
A6 AND A7	MEDIUM BROWN	3/4 YARD	9 STRIPS
A8 AND A9	DARKEST BROWN	1 YARD	14 STRIPS

2nd Color- CREAM BLOCKS - 2 1/2 wide by WOF

A1	DARKEST RED	1/4 YARD	2 STRIPS
A2 AND A3	OFF WHITE	1/2 YARD	5 STRIPS
A4 AND A5	CREAM	1/2 YARD	7 STRIPS
A6 AND A7	BEIGE	3/4 YARD	9 STRIPS
A8 AND A9	TAUPE	1 YARD	14 STRIPS

INNER BOARDER 1/2 YARD- THIS IS QUILTERS CHOICE. USE A COLOR TO FRAME YOUR BLOCKS. I USED THE DARKEST COLOR. THERE IS NO WRONG CHOICE.

CUT INTO 8 STRIPS - 2 INCH WIDTH

• **OUTER BOARDER 1 YARD**

CUT INTO 8 STRIPS - 3 INCHES WIDE
OR- If you have left over strips, sew them in the same strata as the quilt, cut them 3 inch wide sections and
sew them end to end. Now you have a piano key boarder.

• **STABILIZER 5 YARDS OR 3—60 INCH BY WOF SECTIONS**

• **6 YARDS BACKING**

• **1/2 YARD MINKY BINDING (cut 8 strips - 2 inch wide by WOF)**

The quarter square log cabin block uses two different color strata. Each color strata will have 4 shades in that color family from light to dark. The darkest color is repeated in the center. For example: lightest cream or off white, medium cream, beige and taupe with the darkest (red) also being used in the center.

Sub cut the fusible Pelon stabilizer into 3 - 60 inch long sections or pieces. You will then need to sub cut the 60 inch long pieces lengthwise. Sub cut the stabilizer 1/2 to 3/4 wide by the 60 inch length. Don't stress about this part, these pieces will be inside your quilt and nobody will ever see them. We need a lot of pieces so cut all 3 pieces into strips. If you are cutting the length of the stabilizer there will not be any stretch.

Make 32 quarter square blocks of the brown strata and 32 quarter square blocks of the blue strata. Each strip must have a strip of stabilizer ironed on the wrong side down each edge. See photo.

When you place your strips of Minky fabric together they have a tendency to slide. Always pin the beginning and end of each piece. You can also finger press the edges together as you sew. This also helps keep the edges from slipping. The trick is to allow the machine to feed the fabric through the feed dogs but keep enough pressure to hold the fabric together. If you have a walking foot for your machine, use it.

Stabilizer Ironed onto each edge of wrong side Press the edge together as of each strip as you

sew keeps the edges from slipping or you can pin.

 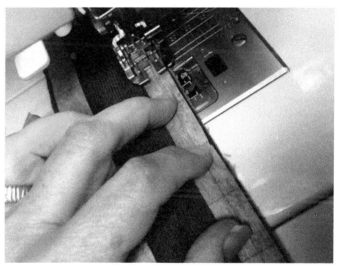

1. Take your **A1 color strip** and the **A2 color strip** and sew them together along the edge. This will give you a unit of 4 1/2 inches by 60 inches. Make 2 units of these.

2. Sub cut this first unit (A1 + A2) into 2 /12 wide pieces. Repeat until you have 32 blocks. Press open the seam using a presser sheet. After the first two strips are connected and then sub cut, sew on the *A3 strip* to the left side of the unit. Keep in mind, all the strips will be added to the left side or the top. You can chain sew these units together as shown below. The last example of chain piecing shows that if you don't keep the units abutted that you might have to trim twice. Don't stress, I frequently have to trim twice.

Chain Piecing

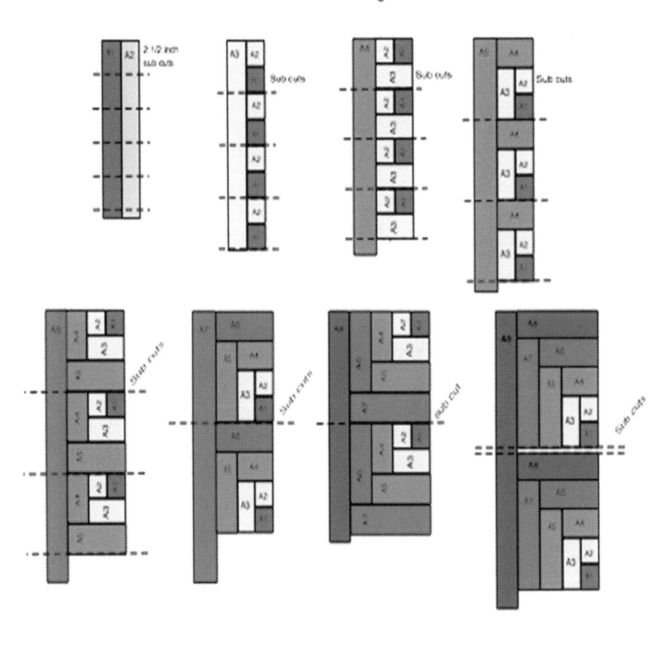

Outer Border

Make sure your outer border pieces have been prepared with stabilizer. Just like the inner border, sew two pieces end to end. Make 4 units.

Measure your sides, cut two side pieces (93 3/4 inches). Pin in place and sew. Press open using presser sheet.

Measure the top and bottom, cut the two remaining border pieces to fit (99 1/4 inches). Pin and sew, press open seam allowances with presser sheet.

Wow, great job!! STAND BACK AND LOOK AT THE AMAZING JOB YOU DID!

QUARTER SQUARE LOG CABIN - Oversized Queen

Here are two different log cabins using a similar color strata but I changed one from a light center to a dark center just to achieve a different look. I used some of the left over strips to make a striped border instead of smooth border.

Quarter Square

Log Cabin Lap Quilt

Material List

3/4 yard Navy Minky

3/4 yard Mango Yellow Minky

2/3 yard Royal Blue Minky

2/3 yard Limon Yellow Minky

1/3 yard Electric Blue Minky

1/3 yard Canary Yellow Minky

1/4 yard Dusty Blue Minky

1/4 yard Yellow Minky

1 yard Electric Blue - border

3/4 yard Dusty Blue - binding (optional)

4 yards backing

5 yards Fusible Lightweight Pelon Stabilizer

6 x 36 Minky Ruler

Presser sheet

Thread to match

Roller Cutter

QUARTER SQUARE LOG CABIN-LAP QUILT

Number Of Strips

BLUE BLOCKS - All strips for the blocks are 2 1/2 inches wide by WOF

A1	DUSTY BLUE	1/4 YARD	2 STRIPS
A2 AND A3	ELECTRIC BLUE	1/3 YARD	4 STRIPS
A4 AND A5	ROYAL BLUE	2/3 YARD	7 STRIPS
A6 AND A7	NAVY BLUE	3/4 YARD	8 STRIPS

YELLOW BLOCKS - All strips for the blocks are 2 1/2 wide by WOF

A1	LIGHTEST YELLOW	1/4 YARD	2 STRIPS
A2 AND A3	CANARY YELLOW	1/3 YARD	4 STRIPS
A4 AND A5	LIMON YELLOW	2/3 YARD	7 STRIPS
A6 AND A7	MANGO YELLOW	2/3 YARD	8 STRIPS

- **BORDER 1 YARD**

CUT INTO 6 STRIPS - 5 1/2 INCHES WIDE by WOF (SET ASIDE)

- **SUB CUT - STABILIZER 5 YARDS INTO 3—60 INCH BY WOF SECTIONS**

SUB CUT AGAIN- 3/4 INCH WIDE BY THE 60 INCH LENGTH.

The QUARTER SQUARE LOG CABIN BLOCK uses two different color strata. Each color strata will have 4 shades in that color family. For example, lightest blue, medium blue, medium dark blue and darkest blue. The second block will have the lightest yellow, medium yellow, medium dark yellow and darkest yellow.

After you have prepared each of the strips with a stabilizer on each edge, you need to pin. Either pin a lot or use this little trick. Press you fingers along the edge as the material is fed through the feed dogs, this keeps the fabric from slipping and sliding but still allows the sewing machine to feed the fabric through the feed dogs. Using a walking foot on your machine makes this a little easier. Sew with a 1/4 inch seam allowance.

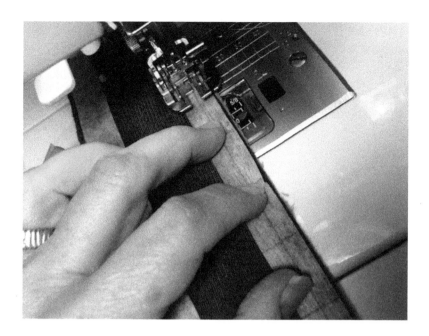

Make 24 Blue strata Quarter Square blocks and 24 Yellow strata Quarter Square blocks. Before you begin to sew, all strips must have a stabilizer strip ironed on to the wrong side on each edge. The photo shows the correct placement of the stabilizer strip and finger pressing technique.

USE A 1/4 INCH SEAM ALLOWANCE

Take the A1 color strip and A2 color strip and sew them together along their full length using

1/4 inch seam allowance. When these two are sewn together you will have a 4 1/2 wide

by 60 inch long unit. Make two of these. Press seams open with presser sheet.

Sub cut this first unit into 2 1/2 inch wide pieces. You will have a 2 1/2 inch wide by 4 1/2 wide piece. Continue to sub cut this unit until you have 24 blocks. Look at the block layout provided. After the first two strips are connected you will just repeat with the next strip which would be A3, then A4 and so on. Chain piecing directions show the progression of adding additional strips. Press all Seams open with presser sheet.

Chain Piecing - Lap Quilt Directions

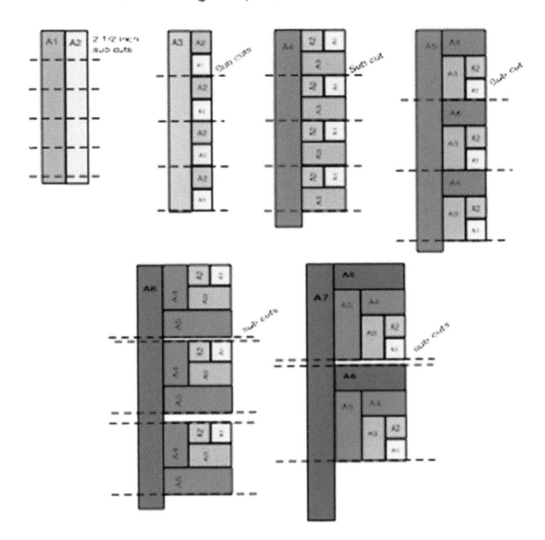

1. Chain Piecing diagram shows sub cut lines. The last two groups show a double cut line. This happens when you don't get the block perfectly touching the previous block. Don't worry, it happens, it is important to make the second cut and keep the blocks as square as possible.

2. Follow the BLOCK LAYOUT to keep track of which strip comes next. You could write the color of your strips on the block layout to remind you which color is next.

3. After you have all 24 blocks of one color strata completed, set them aside and repeat step 1, 2 and 3 until you have 24 blocks of the second color strata.

4. Follow the block placement at the beginning of this quilt direction

5. The finished blocks will be 9 3/4 square (about), this always depends if you used a 1/4 inch seam allowance.

6. Lay the blocks out according to the diagram and sew them together. Press seams open using a presser sheet.

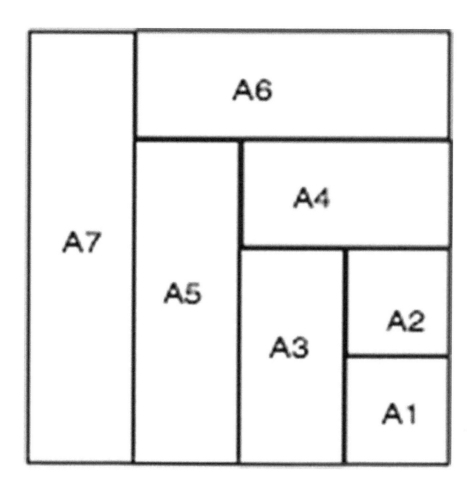

Quarter Square Log Cabin - Lap Quilt Strip Diagram

You can use this template to write you color selections or tape a piece of your fabric in the corresponding strip. This is an opportunity to see how your colors will look before you sew.

Make sure you have already ironed on the fusible stabilizer strips to the wrong sides of the border pieces. Cut two of the 5 1/2 inch wide by WOF border pieces in half. This will create 4 pieces. Iron on a stabilizer strip along the cut edge of each piece. Sew one of these pieces onto one of the full length border piece. Repeat to all 4. Now you should have 4 border pieces that are 5 1/2 inches by 90 inches.

Measure the length of your quilt. You should have 74 3/4 inches (about). Cut two of your border pieces to the length of your quilt (74 3/4 inches) Pin and sew on the side border pieces. Press open seams.

Measure the top and bottom width. Width should be 66 1/4 (about). Cut the remaining two border pieces to fit your quilt. Pin and sew on the top and bottom borders.

Western Montana Landscape

Materials

1 yard landscape"minky"   5 yards fusible Pelon Stabilizer

1 1/2 yard navy embossed arrow "minky" 4 yards backing

1/3 yard latte "minky" Presser sheet

1/2 yard tan arrow "minky" Matching thread

1/2 yard buffalo skull "minky"

1/2 yard rain "minky"

Use pressing sheet to press open all seams. Sew using 1/4 inch seam allowance.

Fusible Pelon Stabilizer-

Sub cut the fusible Pelon stabilizer into 3 - 60 inch long sections or pieces. You will then need to sub cut the 60 inch long pieces lengthwise. Sub cut the stabilizer 1/2 to 3/4 wide by the 60 inch length. Don't stress about this part, these pieces will be inside your quilt and nobody will ever see them. We need a lot of pieces so cut all 3 pieces into strips. If you are cutting the length of the stabilizer there will not be any stretch.

As you are cutting the big blocks for this quilt, remember to iron on the stabilizer strips on the wrong side one each of the edges.

Western Montana Landscape Minky Cutting Directions

LANDSCAPE MINKY -

CUT 2 - 18 1/2 inch X 28 1/2 inch pieces

CUT 2- 8 1/2 inch by 14 1/2 inch pieces

CUT 2 - 6 1/2 inch strips, prepare with stabilizer strips on the wrong side, alone each edge

- SUB-CUT 10- 6 1/2 X 6 1/2 inch squares - iron on fusible stabilizer to the newly cut sides.

NAVY EMBOSSED ARROW "MINKY"

CUT - 6 - 4 1/2 inch strips by (WOF) Prepare the strips with fusible stabilizer along each edge and then set aside for outer border.

CUT 1 - 6 1/2 inch wide by WOF-

Before you sub cut - iron on the fusible stabilizer along each edge, then after you sub cut the pieces you will need to iron on the fusible stabilizer on the remaining edges.

- SUBCUT the 6 1/2 inch wide strip into 9— 6 1/2 IN X 6 1/2 squares

LATTE "MINKY"

CUT - 3 pieces- 2 1/2 inch wide by WOF - prepare with fusible stabilizer strips along each edge before sub-cut.

From the 2 1/2 wide pieces Sub-cut:

- SUB-CUT- 4 - 2 1/2 inch by 28 1/2 inch pieces

- SUB-CUT- 2- 2 1/2 inch by 32 1/2 inch pieces

- SUB-CUT- 4 - 2 1/2 inch by 14 1/2 inch pieces

- SUB-CUT- 4 - 2 1/2 inch by 12 1/2 inch pieces

CUT — 2 - 1 1/2 INCH BY WOF

- SUB-CUT **2** - 1 1/2 inch by 30 1/2 inch pieces

TAN ARROW "MINKY"

CUT - 2 - 6 1/2 inch wide by WOF strips -prepare with fusible stabilizer strips along each edge before you sub cut.

- SUB-CUT 10 - 6 1/2 BY 6 1/2 inch squares. Iron on fusible stabilizer on each of the cut edges

BUFFALO SKULL "MINKY"

CUT 2 - 6 1/2 inch by WOF strips- prepare with fusible stabilizer strips along each edge before you sub cut.

- SUB -CUT—10 - 6 1/2 inch by 6 1/2 inch squares. Iron on fusible stabilizer on each of the cut edges

NAVY/WHITE RAIN "MINKY"

SUBCUT 1 - 6 1/2 inch by WOF strip - prepare with fusible stabilizer strips along each edge before you sub cut.

- SUB-CUT— 9 - 6 1/2 BY 6 1/2 inch squares. Iron on fusible stabilizer on each of the cut edges.

Left side of quilt layout

row 1

latte 2 1/2 x 28 1/2	latte 2 1/2 x 32 1/2

focal fabric panel
18 1/2 x 28 1/2

latte 2 1/2 x 28 1/2

row 2

focal	buffalo skull	rain	navy arrows	tan arrows

row 3

buffalo skull		latte 2 1/2 x 12 1/2	latte 2 1/2 x 18 1/2	latte 2 1/2 x 12 1/2	focal
rain			focal fabric 8 1/2 x 18 1/2		buffalo skull
			latte 2 1/2 x 18 1/2		

row 4

navy arrows	tan arrows	focal	buffalo skull	rain
tan arrows	focal	buffalo skull	rain	navy arrows
focal	buffalo skull	rain	navy arrows	tan arrows

row 5

latte 1 1/2 x 30 1/2

Right side of Quilt layout

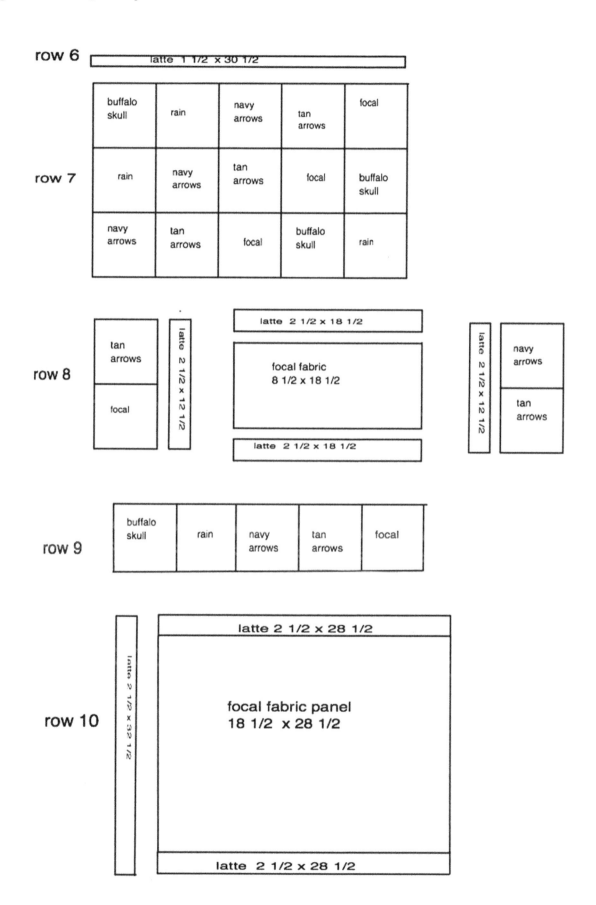

row 6
latte 1 1/2 x 30 1/2

buffalo skull	rain	navy arrows	tan arrows	focal
rain	navy arrows	tan arrows	focal	buffalo skull
navy arrows	tan arrows	focal	buffalo skull	rain

row 7

row 8

tan arrows

focal

latte 2 1/2 x 12 1/2

latte 2 1/2 x 18 1/2

focal fabric
8 1/2 x 18 1/2

latte 2 1/2 x 18 1/2

latte 2 1/2 x 12 1/2

navy arrows

tan arrows

row 9

buffalo skull	rain	navy arrows	tan arrows	focal

row 10

latte 2 1/2 x 32 1/2

latte 2 1/2 x 28 1/2

focal fabric panel
18 1/2 x 28 1/2

latte 2 1/2 x 28 1/2

Western Montana Landscape

Finished sized 67.5 x 73

4 1/2 x 73 navy arrows

4 X 59 1/2 navy arrows

4 1/2 x 59 1/2 navy arrow

latte 2 1/2 x 28 1/2

focal fabric panel
18 1/2 x 28 1/2

latte 2 1/2 x 28 1/2

latte 2 1/2 x 32 1/2

latte 1 1/2 x 30 1/2

buffalo skull	rain	navy arrows	tan arrows	focal
rain	navy arrows	tan arrows	focal	buffalo skull
navy arrows	tan arrows	focal	buffalo skull	rain

latte 2 1/2 x 59 1/2

focal	buffalo skull	rain	navy arrows	tan arrows
buffalo skull				
rain				

latte 2 1/2 x 14 1/2

focal fabric
8 1/2 x 14 1/2

latte 2 1/2 x 12 1/2

latte 2 1/2 x 14 1/2

navy arrows	tan arrows	focal	buffalo skull	rain
tan arrows	focal	buffalo skull	rain	navy arrows
focal	buffalo skull	rain	navy arrows	tan arrows

tan arrows

focal

latte 2 1/2 x 14 1/2

focal fabric
8 1/2 x 14 1/2

latte 2 1/2 x 12 1/2

latte 2 1/2 x 14 1/2

navy arrows

tan arrows

| buffalo skull | rain | navy arrows | tan arrows | focal |

latte 2 1/2 x 32 1/2

latte 2 1/2 x 28 1/2

focal fabric panel
18 1/2 x 28 1/2

latte 2 1/2 x 28 1/2

latte 1 1/2 x 30 1/2

4 1/2 x 73 navy arrows

30

Turtle Applique instructions

Increase size to 150% of orginal

Trace each of the turtle pieces onto fusible pellon stabilizer, don't cut the pieces out yet.

Iron the traced pieces onto the wrong side of minky.

Now you can cut out the body parts.

Pin the turtle parts onto the quilt and sew straight stitch around the outlines. Sew the texture lines onto the turtle shell, the eye outlines and lines on the turtle fins.

Use fabric markers to outline the textures on the fins and turtle face. This gives so much more depth. Make sure your markers are fabric permanent markers.

Make as many baby turtles as you like, this is the fun part to make it your own.

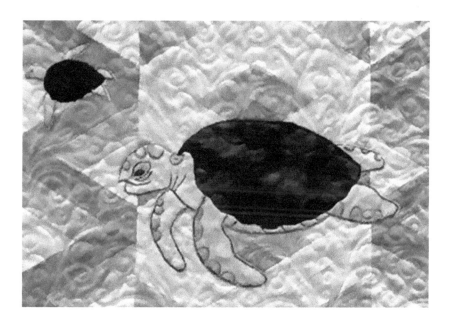

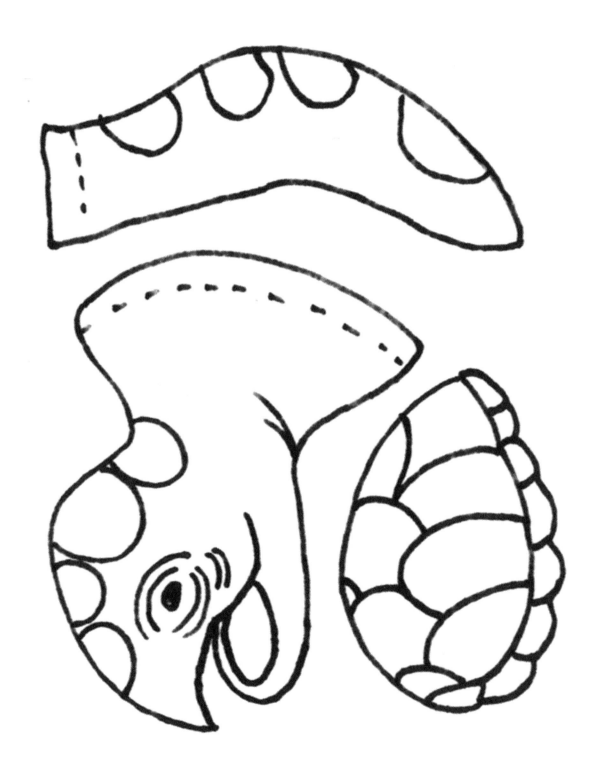

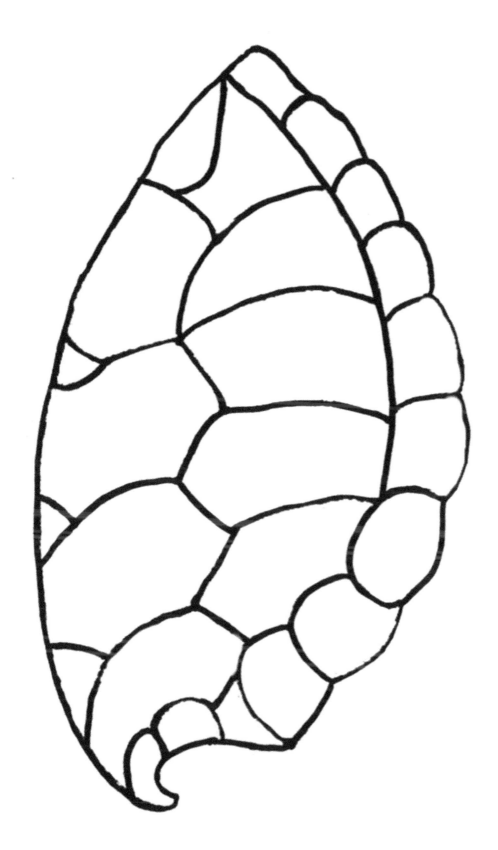

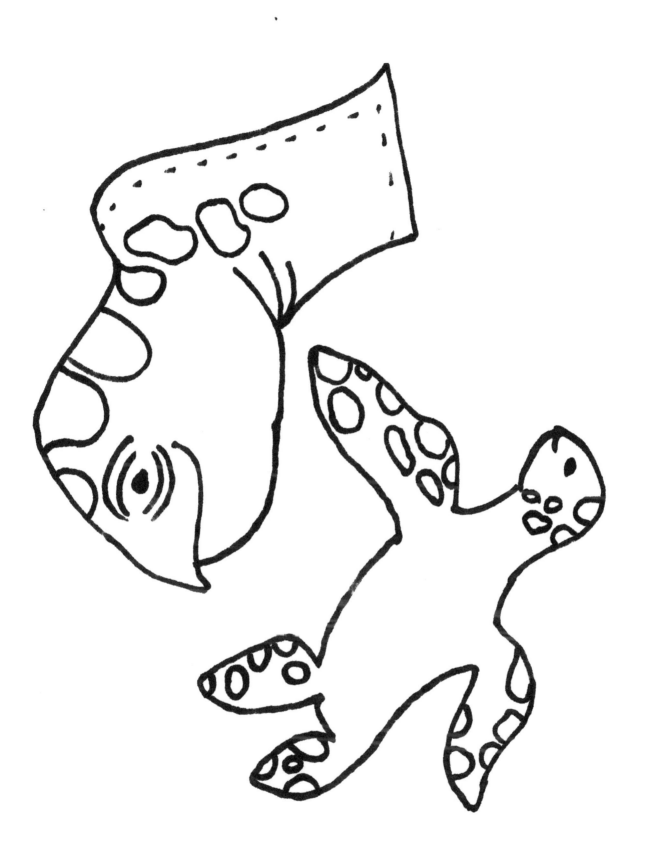

Northern Lights Applique Pieces.

The trunk of the tree is a 3 inch by 60 inch strip of black **Minky**. The top 18 inches of that piece should be tapered to 1 inch wide. If you make a mark 18 inch from the top of the strip and draw a line angling to the top will give you a really nice tapered tree. Make the same mark on the other side and angle to the center of the top.

Place the tree trunk so that it is highlighted by the lighter colored quilt pieces. This helps the tree look like it is on the horizon. Pin the edges so it stays in place. Now take the branches, make the long or short but vary their placement. Tuck the branches under the tree trunk and pin them in place.

Branch Placement

1 Inch

Cut Line

Top 18 inches of the tree trunk

3 inch

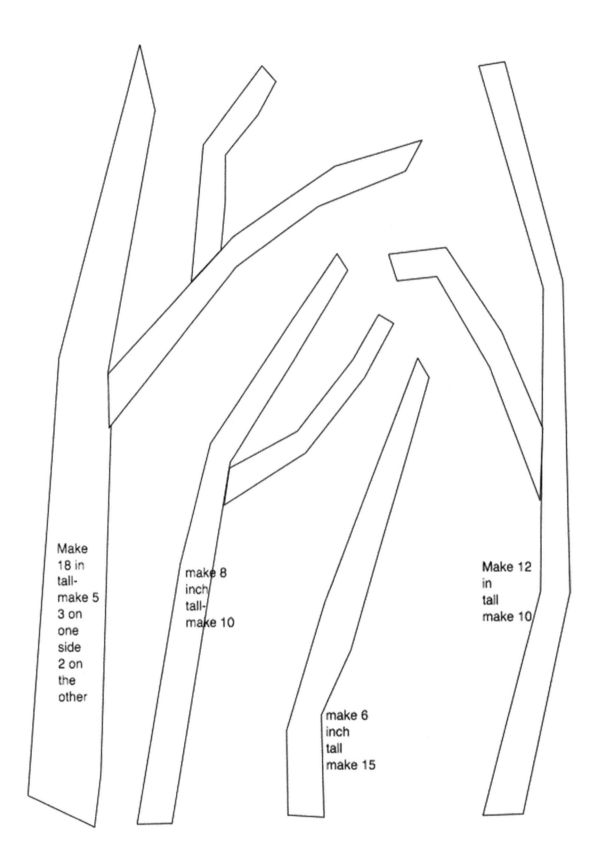

Make
18 in
tall-
make 5
3 on
one
side
2 on
the
other

make 8
inch
tall-
make 10

Make 12
in
tall
make 10

make 6
inch
tall
make 15

CPSIA information can be obtained
at www.ICGtesting.com
Printed in the USA
BVHW02s0958190918
527925BV00011B/89/P